Beyond
The
Divine Beads

Author
Pragati Mukherjee

RIDHZWORLD
PUBLISHING

AF516992

COPYRIGHT © 2025 BY Pragati Mukherjee

All rights reserved. No part of this publication may be reproduced, stored in or introduced into a retrieval system, or transmitted, in any form, or by any means (electronic, mechanical, photocopying, recording or otherwise) without the prior written permission of the publisher. Any person who does any unauthorized act in relation to this publication may be liable to criminal prosecution and civil claims for damages.

This book is sold subject to the condition that it shall not, by way of trade or otherwise, be lent, re-sold, hired out, or otherwise circulated without the publisher's prior consent in any form of binding or cover other than that in which it is published and without a similar condition including this condition being imposed on the subsequent purchaser.

Please do not participate in or encourage piracy of copyrighted materials in violation of the author's rights. Purchase only authorized editions.

First Printing Edition @ 2025
Paperback ISBN: 978-81-986982-2-3
eBook ISBN: 978-81-986982-8-5

Published

by

RidhzWorld Publishing
Hadapsar, Pune, India
https://www.ridhzworld.com

Table of Contents

Preface

In a world increasingly seeking balance amidst chaos, the ancient wisdom of Rudraksha offers a path to inner peace and well-being. A simple bead born from nature, yet imbued with immense spiritual and scientific value. This book is not just a guide but a heartfelt exploration of the Rudraksha's journey from the sacred legends of Lord Shiva to its modern-day.

From the mystical origins in Lord Shiva's tears to its scientifically recognized electromagnetic properties, Rudraksha beads have been revered for centuries as powerful tools for spiritual growth, emotional stability, and physical vitality.

This work is a product of deep personal interest and passion, drawn from various authentic sources available through published literature and reputable online research. It does not claim to be scholarly but aims to present the subject in a simple, accessible way for those embarking on their own spiritual path or simply wishing to understand the mystery behind these sacred beads.

As you turn the pages, may this book serve as a quiet companion, one that connects you to the roots of nature, the stillness within, and the divine energy that Rudraksha has symbolized for millennia.

Chapter 1 – Introduction to Rudraksha

Elaeocarpus ganitrus Roxb, commonly known as Rudraksha, are the ancient beads of wisdom that hold the secrets of bringing out the unique discoveries of this vibrant universe. Its origin being from the striking Rudraksh tree, these powerful Rudraksh beads have been passed on across various cultures and traditions for centuries. The Rudraksha trees are found in Southeast Asia, Nepal, as well as the mountainous regions of the Himalayas. In Sanskrit, it is known as *Rudraksha* and in Tamil it is known as *Aakkam.*

"Rudra" referring to Lord Shiva himself, and "Aksha" meaning tears; hence Rudraksha being the tears of Lord Shiva, have been worn by many yogis and spiritual seekers to receive energies beyond the human mind and soul. The sacred beads have been scientifically proven to reduce mental stress and anxiety, promoting emotional balance and spiritual growth.

Rudraksha is the fruit (stone) of the *E. ganitrus Roxb.* If we see it from a scientific point of view, then the outer covering of the Rudraksha has several medicinal values like boiling them in water and drinking it to cure fever, cold, and cough. The leaves are believed to have antibacterial properties and are used in treating wounds. The beads have seeds inside, and it receives nourishment from its central cavity.

Introduction to Rudraksha

Elaeocarpus ganitrus Roxb

Commonly known as Rudraksha, the ancient beads of wisdom originating from a Rudraksha tree

Originating from Tears of Lord Shiva

Reduces stress, anxiety and promote spiritual growth

The Legacy and Importance

Sacred beads worn for centuries, valued for their spiritual, emotional, and health benefits

Shape and Size

Varies in size from 5mm to over 25mm

Color

Naturally appear in white, red, yellow, and black

Typically, round or oval with a rough surface and natural lines known as "Mukhis".

Why Rudraksha Still Matters Today

As a tool for personal wellbeing

Universal Tool

Ideal for Personal Wellbeing

The Legacy and Importance of Rudraksha

Rudraksha is not just a spiritual symbol; it is a bridge connecting the natural world, ancient traditions, and modern wellness practices. Across centuries, sages, saints, and seers have used these beads during meditation, believing that Rudraksha helps to align one's inner self with the cosmic energy. Even today, millions wear them for their believed abilities to enhance focus, calm the mind, and protect against negative influences.

Modern studies suggest that Rudraksha may influence the bio-electric field of the human body. This interaction is said to bring harmony to the nervous system, stabilize heartbeat, and even have a positive effect on blood pressure levels. These holistic benefits make Rudraksha a fascinating object of both faith and science.

Shape and Size

Rudraksha beads are typically round or oval. Their size can vary significantly, ranging from small (around 5 mm) to large (upwards of 25–35 mm), depending on their origin. Nepali Rudraksha beads tend to be larger than those from Indonesia.

The most distinguishing feature is the presence of natural lines or clefts running vertically from one end to the other. These lines create segments or facets on the bead's surface, known as "Mukhis" (faces). The number of Mukhis can range from one to twenty-one (and very rarely even more). Each Mukhi has its own significance and is associated with different deities and energies.

The surface of a genuine Rudraksha bead is usually rough and uneven, similar to a walnut shell. It has a natural, unpolished feel. The most common color is brown, ranging from light to dark shades. However, Rudraksha beads can also be found in white, red, yellow, or black, although these are less common.

A natural central hole runs through the bead, allowing it to be strung into a mala (rosary) or worn as a pendant. This feature makes Rudraksha not only a spiritual object but also a functional and wearable piece that integrates seamlessly into daily life.

Color

According to ancient Hindu texts, or *Pauranik* versions, Rudraksha seeds (from the *Elaeocarpus ganitrus Roxb* tree) are described as having four colors: white, red, yellow, and black. This color-based sorting is said to occur naturally, influenced by the seed's ripeness, the specific type of tree, and where it grows.

However, trying to categorize Rudraksha by color in practice is challenging because there aren't any standard color definitions, and the shades often blend together. Additionally, scientific research hasn't organized its findings based on the color of the Rudraksha. It seems likely that Rudraksha of any initial color might produce similar effects.

Over time, typically after wearing them for a few months, all types of Rudraksha tend to darken to black or deep brown due to interactions with body oils and perspiration. Consequently, any classification based on color is probably not very useful.

People who strongly adhere to this color-based system, as it's mentioned in religious epics, are free to continue doing so, as it doesn't affect others' beliefs. While traditional texts recommend that Brahmins wear "white" Rudraksha, Kshatriyas "red," Vaishyas "yellow," and Shudras "black," this practice isn't widely followed for several reasons. From a practical standpoint, this color-based classification has very little acceptance.

Why Rudraksha Still Matters Today

Today's generation often seeks inner peace, mindfulness, and emotional stability in an increasingly stressful world. Rudraksha beads, through their historical and energetic significance, provide a unique path toward personal well-being. Wearing Rudraksha is not limited by age, caste, or religion—it's a universal tool for those seeking balance between body, mind, and spirit.

Rudraksha is not about blind belief. It is a convergence of ancient insight and contemporary relevance, a symbol of how our ancestors' discoveries continue to guide modern life.

Looking Ahead – Beyond Mythological Roots

Beyond its mythological roots, Rudraksha's significance extends into the knowledge of science and spirituality. It is also important to understand that Rudraksha's benefits are as diverse as its wearers. As we explore further, the intersection of ancient wisdom and modern understanding will reveal the profound impact of Rudraksha in our lives.

In the coming chapters, we'll delve deeper into the types of Rudraksha, the energies they carry, how to choose the right bead for yourself, and the scientific principles that might explain their powerful influence. Whether you're a curious teenager, a spiritual seeker, or someone passionate about Indian traditions, this journey will open up new dimensions of understanding.

Chapter 2 – Legend of Rudraksha

Birthplace

The Himalayan region, particularly the spiritually rich areas of Nepal, Northern India, and Bhutan, is widely revered as the birthplace of Rudraksha—the sacred bead of *Elaeocarpus ganitrus*. This region's unique climate, altitude, and soil composition are believed to contribute to the purity and potency of the Rudraksha trees grown there. More than just a physical origin, this birthplace symbolizes a gateway to the divine, embodying the spiritual essence of the land where sages have meditated and seekers have walked paths of enlightenment for thousands of years.

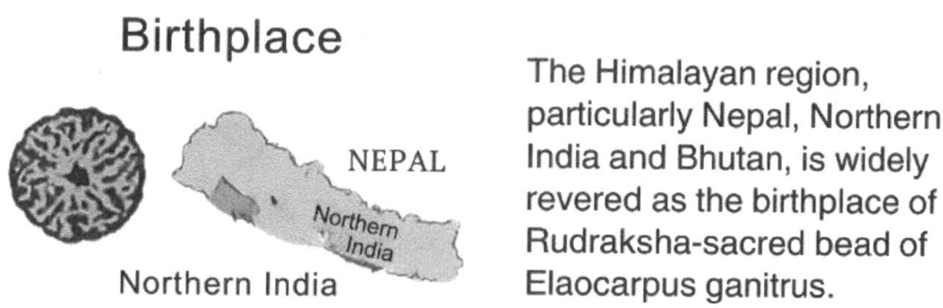

Beads harvested from this region are often regarded as the most powerful and energetically charged, which is why spiritual practitioners around the world prefer Rudraksha from Nepal and the Himalayas.

Mythological Origins

According to ancient scriptures like the Shiva Purana, Shrimad Devi Bhagwat, Padma Purana, and Linga Purana, the origin of Rudraksha is deeply embedded in divine mythology. It is said that Lord Shiva, the supreme yogi, went into deep meditation for thousands of years to protect the world from destructive forces. Overwhelmed by the depth of his compassion and the intensity of his meditation, tears of divine ecstasy flowed from his eyes. These celestial tears fell to the Earth and gave birth to the Rudraksha trees. The seeds from these trees grew into sacred beads that would one day become tools for spiritual awakening, compassion, and expanded consciousness.

Each bead, thus, carries within it the essence of Shiva's compassion and power, making it not just an accessory, but a living relic of divine history.

According to ancient scriptures. Rudraksha originated from the divine tears of Lord Shiva, which fell to Earth and grew into sacred trees.

Symbolism of the Third Eye

The Vedic tradition aligns Rudraksha with the third eye of Lord Shiva—*Ajna Chakra*—the center of intuition, perception, and wisdom. It is believed that wearing Rudraksha helps awaken this inner eye, allowing seekers to access deeper awareness, clarity of thought, and higher states of consciousness. For those who

Symbolism of the Third Eye

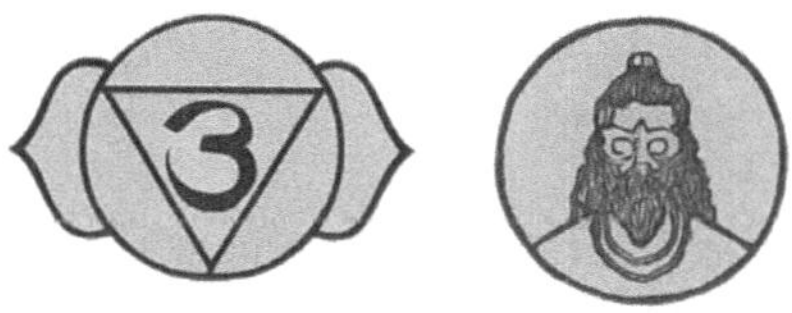

Rudraksha is aligned with Lord Shiva's third eye-Ajna Chakra.

meditate or walk a spiritual path, this connection represents an opportunity to tap into insight beyond logic, to feel rather than simply think.

Vedic Astrology Connection

In Vedic astrology, Rudraksha is not merely symbolic; it is functional. Each type of Rudraksha corresponds to one of the nine planetary influences (Navagrahas) and is believed to harmonize their energies. For instance, wearing a bead aligned with your dominant or afflicted planet can help restore energetic balance, improve emotional resilience, and foster spiritual growth.

Thus, Rudraksha becomes a cosmic tool, allowing individuals to align themselves with the universe's natural rhythms and correct imbalances in their astrological charts.

The Spiritual Design of Rudraksha

The physical structure of Rudraksha beads carries symbolic meaning rooted in spiritual philosophy. If you closely observe a bead:

The Spiritual Design of Rudraksha

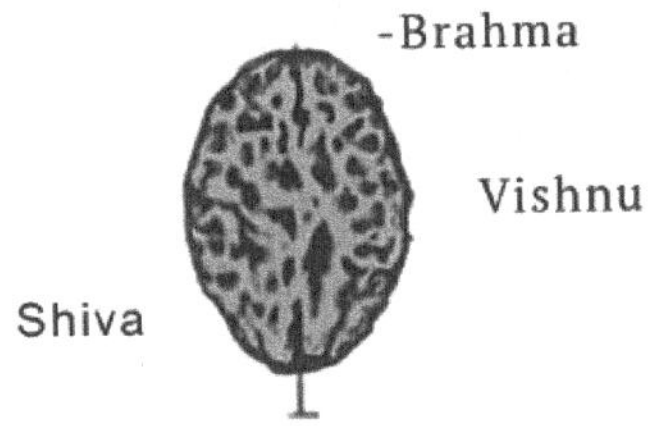

The bead's structure symbolizes the Hindu Trinity (Trimurti)- representing Creation, Preservation, and Destruction

- The top—from where all lines emerge is called Brahma, symbolizing the origin of creation.
- The middle, the widest part, is Vishnu, the preserver.
- The bottom, where all lines converge, is Shiva, the destroyer and transformer.

This triadic structure beautifully represents the Hindu Trinity (Trimurti) and reinforces Rudraksha's status as a microcosmic embodiment of universal energies: Creation, Preservation, and Destruction.

Types of Rudraksha

Interestingly, there are 29 Mukhi Rudraksha varieties discovered in Nepal, and even more have been identified in Indonesian regions. Despite the rarity of these higher-faced beads, 11 types of Mukhi Rudraksha are commonly used in daily life and spiritual practice. These include:

Types of Rudraksha

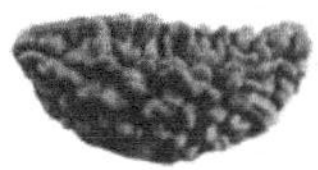

1 Mukhi Rudraksha

2 Mukhi Rudraksha

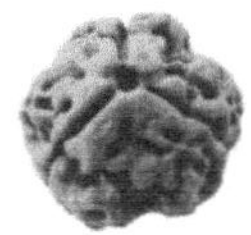

3 Mukhi Rudraksha

4 Mukhi Rudraksha

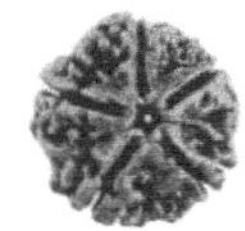

5 Mukhi Rudraksha

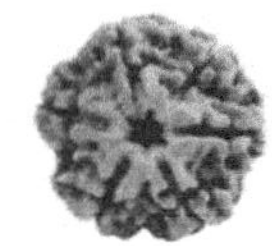

6 Mukhi Rudraksha

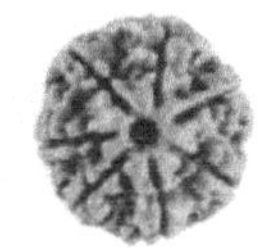

7 Mukhi Rudraksha

8 Mukhi Rudraksha

9 Mukhi Rudraksha

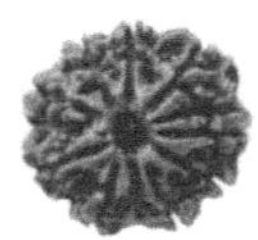

10 Mukhi Rudraksha

11 Mukhi Rudraksha

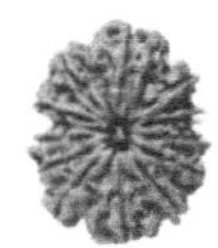

12 Mukhi Rudraksha

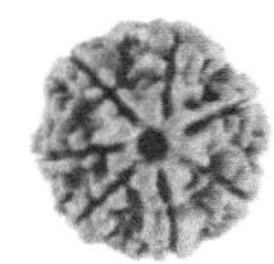

13 Mukhi Rudraksha

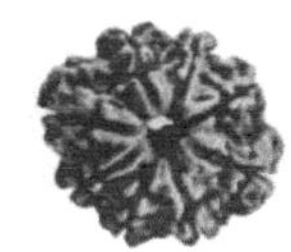

14 Mukhi Rudraksha

1 Face Mukhi Rudraksha Energy

2 Face Mukhi Rudraksha Energy

3 Face Mukhi Rudraksha Energy

4 Face Mukhi Rudraksha Energy

5 Face Mukhi Rudraksha Energy

6 Face Mukhi Rudraksha Energy

7 Face Mukhi Rudraksha Energy

8 Face Mukhi Rudraksha Energy

9 Face Mukhi Rudraksha Energy

10 Face Mukhi Rudraksha Energy

11 Face Mukhi Rudraksha Energy

Each of these carries unique spiritual properties and is believed to invoke different aspects of divine energy, depending on the number of Mukhis (faces) on the bead.

Other Significant and Rare Rudrakshas

While the commonly known Mukhis are widely used, some unique formations of Rudraksha beads hold legendary spiritual significance:

◇ *Garbh Gauri Rudraksha*

This rare bead consists of two naturally joined beads, one significantly smaller than the other. Symbolically, it represents Goddess Parvati (Gauri) and her unborn child Lord Ganesha. It is especially beneficial for:

- Fertility and safe pregnancy
- Strengthening mother-child relationships
- Invoking divine motherly protection

◇ *Gauri Shankar Rudraksha*

Two equal-sized beads fused together, this formation symbolizes the sacred union of Shiva and Parvati. It is believed to:

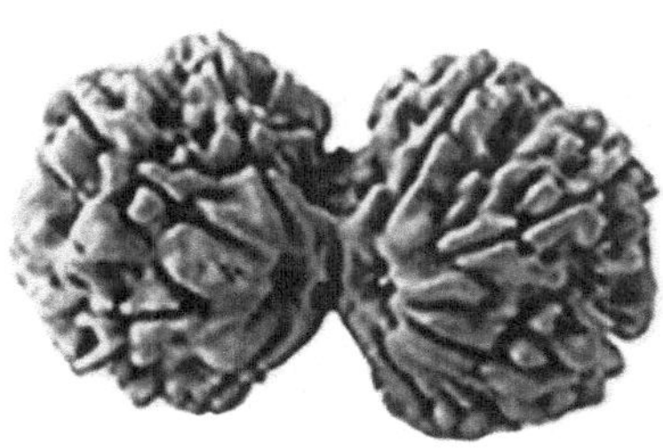

- Enhance love and marital harmony
- Balance masculine and feminine energies
- Deepen spiritual connection between partners

◇ *Trijuti Rudraksha*

A natural fusion of three beads on one stalk, the Trijuti is a rare marvel, representing the Tridev—Brahma, Vishnu, and Shiva. Its powerful vibration is associated with:

- Leadership and strength
- Spiritual mastery
- Protection on all planes

◇ *Savar Naag Rudraksha*

This formation includes a One Mukhi Rudraksha joined with any other bead, often shaped like a cobra's hood—hence the name "Naag". Ruled by Lord Shiva, this Rudraksha is known for:

- Dissolving obstacles
- Boosting courage and clarity
- Supporting material and spiritual success

Bhadraksha: A Word of Caution

There exists another variety called Bhadraksha, originating from trees like *Koenigii*, *Goodeniaceae*, and *Scaevola frutescens*. These seeds:

- Are usually flat, light, and smooth
- Often come as two-faced beads
- Lack a natural hole, unlike genuine Rudraksha

Though occasionally used in rituals, Bhadraksha is considered inferior in quality and is sometimes manipulated or carved to pass off as rare Rudraksha types. Unscrupulous practices include crafting symbols of snakes or Shivalingas onto these beads to imitate authentic one-faced Rudraksha. Awareness is key to avoid falling for these imitations.

Beyond Myth – A Legacy of Spiritual Science

While Rudraksha is often viewed through the lens of myth and devotion, it's also a testament to ancient scientific wisdom. The thoughtful connection between form, function, and energy suggests that ancient cultures had a sophisticated understanding of how nature and consciousness could work in harmony.

In the next chapter, we will explore the scientific and spiritual energies of Rudraksha—and how these beads influence our mind, body, and aura in measurable, tangible ways.

Chapter 3 – Spiritual and Scientific Significance

Rudraksha beads hold a unique place across multiple ancient spiritual traditions, including Hinduism, Buddhism, and Jainism. Revered as sacred objects, these beads serve a dual purpose—functioning both as tools for spiritual practice and as physical reminders of one's inner journey. Whether used for chanting, meditation, or rituals, Rudraksha offers a pathway to focus the mind and elevate spiritual consciousness.

In Hindu customs, Rudraksha beads are especially associated with Lord Shiva. Rituals involving the beads often include offerings, chants, and prayers to Shiva, invoking his divine protection and blessings. Wearing a Rudraksha is considered more than an act of faith—it is believed to be a bridge between the physical and spiritual realms, unlocking inner peace, emotional strength, and spiritual awakening.

Traditionally, Rudraksha beads are strung into malas (garlands) using silk, black, or red cotton threads. A full mala contains 108 beads plus one additional bead, known as the "Meru" or "Guru" bead. The number 108 holds deep symbolic value in Vedic cosmology—it represents the wholeness of existence, tying together cosmic principles and human consciousness. The Guru bead is not counted during mantra chanting but serves as a starting and ending point, signifying the infinite loop of life and learning.

RUDRAKSHA BEADS

SPIRITUAL AND SCIENTIFIC SIGNIFICANCE

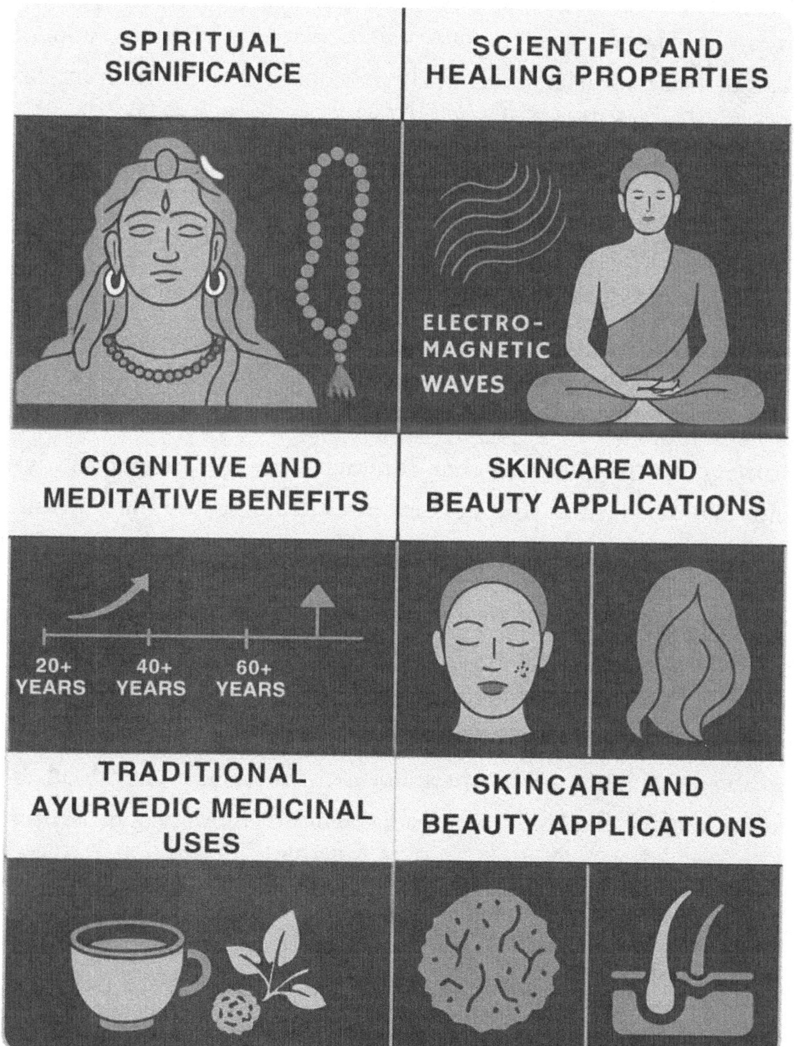

Just like rosaries in Christianity or Tasbih in Islam, a Rudraksha mala is used for Japa, or the repetitive chanting of mantras. The most common mantra, "Om Namah Shivaya," honors Lord Shiva and is believed to cleanse the soul, sharpen focus, and bring spiritual alignment. In later chapters, we will explore how each type of Rudraksha bead is associated with a specific mantra, helping to overcome different life challenges—from fear and stress to physical ailments and emotional instability.

Healing Energies and Scientific Properties

Beyond spiritual practices, Rudraksha beads are renowned for their healing properties—both mental and physical. Modern enthusiasts and ancient sages alike believe that these beads emit unique electromagnetic frequencies that interact with the human body's biofield. These natural frequencies are thought to align bodily energies, reduce stress, and encourage emotional balance.

A commonly practiced ritual involves soaking Rudraksha beads in water overnight and drinking this energized water on an empty stomach. This water is believed to carry bioenergetic qualities that can improve metabolism, boost immunity, and purify the blood. According to ancient recommendations, one should stand on an insulating surface like wool or wood while drinking, to retain the charged particles effectively. Scientifically, the seeds release electrolytes during the soaking process, mildly increasing the water's conductivity—lending a fascinating intersection of tradition and science.

Kirlian Photography: Glimpsing the Energy Field

To explore the mystery of Rudraksha energy visually, some researchers have turned to Kirlian Photography—a process that captures electrical discharges from an object placed on a photographic plate connected to high voltage. This technique, invented by Semyon and Valentina Kirlian in the 1930s, is often used to visualize the "aura" or energy field surrounding living and non-living objects.

When Rudraksha beads are photographed using this method, variations in the color, shape, and brightness of the resulting energy field have been observed. Enthusiasts interpret these images as indicators of a bead's energy potency or purity. However, it's important to note that many factors—such as pressure, moisture, temperature, and electrical strength—can influence these visual results. While intriguing, the study of Kirlian photography still lacks standardized methods and remains a field in development.

Nonetheless, experiments suggest that people in relaxed or meditative states tend to emit larger, whiter auras—indicating a more balanced energy state. Wearing Rudraksha is believed by many to enhance this aura over time, especially with consistent spiritual practice.

Cognitive and Meditative Benefits

One of the most well-documented uses of Rudraksha is in meditation and mindfulness practices. By enhancing concentration, focus, and mental clarity, these beads assist in entering deeper states of meditation. The natural vibrations emitted by Rudraksha are believed to soothe the nervous system, bringing emotional calm and reducing mental chatter.

Modern-day users often report improved memory, sharper focus, and emotional resilience when using Rudraksha consistently. Unlike synthetic tools or supplements, Rudraksha offers a natural and holistic approach to cognitive and emotional health—rooted in centuries of tradition.

Lifespan and Energy Retention

A common question is: *How long does a Rudraksha retain its power?* While the seed within the bead can remain intact for decades—sometimes even a century—its energy potency may vary. Heavier beads often retain more moisture and are believed to be more "alive," while lighter ones may have already dried out.

The outer shell, formed by nature, protects the inner seed and allows energy to be released gradually. When used regularly for spiritual or therapeutic purposes, it's recommended to replace beads every five years for maximum benefit. In the case of water therapy, where beads are soaked overnight, it's advised to change them annually, as prolonged water exposure diminishes their energetic effectiveness. Old beads, however, can still be preserved for ritual use or kept as sacred tokens.

Traditional Medicinal Applications

Rudraksha has been used extensively in Ayurveda, India's ancient medical system. Various parts of the bead—its pulp, bark, and seed—are used in different remedies, often boiled into decoctions known as *quath*. Here are a few traditional uses:

- **Blood Cleanser & Energy Booster:** Grind Rudraksha and boil in water until reduced to a quarter. Mix with honey and consume regularly.
- **Respiratory Support:** Combine Rudraksha, Harad, Adusa bark, and raisins. Boil into a quath and mix with honey for relief from coughs and weakness.
- **Epilepsy Management:** Powdered Rudraksha, when combined with bark or fruit pulp, has been traditionally used to manage seizures.
- **Liver & Digestion Aid:** A potent mixture of herbs like Giloy, Harad, Chitrak, and Rudraksha boiled into a decoction is used for liver disorders and stomach pain.
- **Insect Bite Remedy:** Boiled Rudraksha and Kakoda root concentrate mixed with ghee is traditionally used to counter insect poison effects.

Rudraksha in Natural Skincare and Beauty

Ancient beauty practices have also embraced Rudraksha as a key ingredient in skincare. Its anti-inflammatory and antioxidant properties make it a powerful addition to homemade beauty treatments:

- **Under-Eye Dark Circles:** Mix ground Rudraksha with lime juice and Tulsi extract to reduce puffiness and pigmentation.
- **Eczema and Ringworm:** Combine Rudraksha powder with cow dung and Ganges water to make a healing paste.
- **Glow Enhancer:** Blend Manjistha and Rudraksha powders with honey and ghee for radiant skin.
- **Pimple Treatment:** A paste of red sandalwood, Banyan tree leaves, and jasmine leaves with Rudraksha clears blemishes.
- **Anti-Wrinkle Face Pack:** Mix eight-faced Rudraksha powder with almond powder and rose water for youthful skin.
- **Hair Revitalizer:** A potent mixture of Rudraksha, black soil, Bhringraj, and sugarcane juice, buried for a month and then applied regularly, is believed to restore hair color and encourage growth.

In the chapters ahead, we will dive deeper into each mukhi Rudraksha, decoding their individual powers, mantras, planetary associations, and specific ways they can help one overcome personal, emotional, and physical obstacles. Rudraksha is not merely a seed—it is a sacred ally for those on a journey toward harmony, healing, and higher consciousness.

Chapter 4 - Understanding Energies of Each Rudraksha

The science behind Rudraksha energies lies in the unique molecular and bio-energetic structure of the beads. Modern research reveals that Rudraksha beads possess a distinct bio-energy signature, which interacts dynamically with the wearer's own energy fields — often referred to as the aura or subtle body energies. This profound interaction is believed to positively influence not just the physical body, but also emotional balance and spiritual growth.

In this chapter, we will explore both the spiritual symbolism and scientific significance of the 11 types of Rudraksha beads. Each bead features its own distinct *Mukhi* (face or segment), and through these faces, divine blessings from various forms of Lord Shiva and other deities are said to flow, channeling specific energies to the wearer.

1 Mukhi Rudraksha

The 1 Mukhi Rudraksha, also called *Eka Mukhi* or *Ekaksha*, is regarded as the holiest and rarest of all Rudraksha beads, primarily found in Nepal and Indonesia. Its energy is connected deeply with Lord Shiva's third eye, symbolizing spiritual awakening, heightened intuition, and ultimate enlightenment.

Typically, the 1 Mukhi Rudraksha is oval and slightly flat, but some natural variations exist. Occasionally, round beads with only one visible face may appear, often from underdeveloped fruit. Even if

X-ray scans reveal multiple internal sections, many still consider these authentic 1 Mukhi beads due to their spiritual potency.

Wearing the *Eka Mukhi* is said to cleanse the wearer's sins, facilitate *Moksha* (liberation from the cycle of birth and death), and aid in managing stressful or challenging situations. Physically, it is believed to help with headaches, eye disorders, skin ailments, and liver-related illnesses.

Mantras for Ekaksha Rudraksha:

Om Namah Shivaya

Om Om Drushaan Namah

Om Hreem Namah

Mahamrityunjaya Mantra

Om Rudra

2 Mukhi Rudraksha

The 2 Mukhi Rudraksha embodies the divine union of masculine and feminine energies, linked to Lord *Ardhanarishvara* — the half-male, half-female form of Lord Shiva. Found in Nepal, Indonesia, as well as the Haridwar and Dehradun regions of India, these beads vary in size and texture depending on their origin.

Nepalese 2 Mukhi beads tend to be flat, smooth, and dense, measuring around 15 mm long. Haridwar and Dehradun varieties are larger, oval, and lighter with a rougher surface. Indonesian 2

Mukhi Rudrakshas are smaller but denser and smoother, featuring two natural internal seeds.

Spiritually, the 2 Mukhi Rudraksha is revered for enhancing harmony and love in relationships, especially between married couples. It is believed to bring peace and improve familial bonds, much like the sacred fire rituals (*Yagnas* or *Homas*) that purify and bless.

Mantras for 2 Mukhi Rudraksha:

Om Namah Shivaya

Om Namah

Om Om Namah

Om Khum

Om Shreem Namah

Mahamrityunjaya Mantra

3 Mukhi Rudraksha

The 3 Mukhi Rudraksha connects with Lord *Agni*, the fire deity and the third form of Lord Shiva, symbolizing purification and transformation through fire. It is believed to burn away sins from past lives, bringing renewal.

Health-wise, the 3 Mukhi bead is said to support treatment of high blood pressure, diabetes, digestive disorders, fever, and even eye problems. Some also suggest it helps guard against serious illnesses such as cancer. Spiritually, it strengthens personal power, encourages positive transformation, and fosters purification of the mind and soul.

People struggling with self-doubt, laziness, or feelings of inferiority often find this Rudraksha beneficial in boosting confidence and motivation.

Mantras for 3 Mukhi Rudraksha:

Om Namah Shivaya

Om Kleem Namah

Om Om Namah

Om Dhum Dhum Namah

Mahamrityunjaya Mantra

4 Mukhi Rudraksha

The 4 Mukhi Rudraksha is widely available, especially from Nepal, and is one of the most commonly used beads. Indonesian varieties tend to be smaller and are often used in prayer malas. Notably, as the number of faces decreases, the beads tend to shift from round to more oval shapes.

This bead is associated with Lord *Brahma*, representing creativity, wisdom, and knowledge — qualities essential for mental clarity and intellectual growth.

Those engaged in mentally demanding work or students seeking better concentration are especially encouraged to wear the 4 Mukhi Rudraksha, as it is believed to enhance memory, focus, and creative thinking.

A traditional practice involves boiling the 4 Mukhi Rudraksha in milk for 10-15 minutes and drinking it, which is said to improve memory and help with memory loss.

4 and 5/6 Mukhi Rudrakshas are often worn together for stress relief and mental health therapy, known as Crown Therapy.

Mantras for 4 Mukhi Rudraksha:

Om Namah Shivaya

Om Hreem Namah

Om Hreem

Om Hreem Hoom Namah

Mahamrityunjaya Mantra

5 Mukhi Rudraksha

The 5 Mukhi Rudraksha, also known as *Pancha Mukhi*, symbolizes the five sacred forms of Lord Shiva: *Sadyojaat, Ishaan, Tatpurush, Aghor,* and *Vaamdev.* These correspond to the five fundamental elements — earth, water, fire, air, and ether — that make up the universe and our very existence.

This bead is the most commonly found Rudraksha, constituting about 60-70% of all beads harvested. Sizes vary depending on origin; Nepalese beads are generally larger (15-30 mm), while Indonesian beads tend to be smaller (4-15 mm). The five natural grooves or *mukh* are clearly visible, dividing the bead into five distinct sections.

The Pancha Mukhi Rudraksha holds immense spiritual significance. In the *Bhagavad Gita*, Lord Krishna teaches Arjuna about focus, determination, and mental clarity amidst turmoil. Similarly, this Rudraksha is believed to enhance mental strength, emotional stability, and spiritual growth, helping the wearer overcome fear, doubt, and distractions.

Physiologically, the human body has seven energy centers called *chakras* that influence physical, emotional, and spiritual well-being. The Pancha Mukhi Rudraksha is thought to harmonize these chakras, especially resonating with the throat chakra — the center of communication, truth, and self-expression. Wearing this bead can empower one to communicate authentically and connect more deeply with others.

Astrologically, the 5 Mukhi Rudraksha is linked with the planet Jupiter (*Guru*), the planet of wisdom, growth, and spiritual awakening. Wearing it is believed to align the wearer with Jupiter's benevolent energies.

In *Vastu Shastra*, placing a Pancha Mukhi Rudraksha in the entrance or workspace is said to ward off negative energies, creating a peaceful and balanced environment.

Ayurveda recognizes the Rudraksha's ability to absorb *Prana* — cosmic life energy — which it then transmits to the wearer. This helps calm the nervous system, balance the *doshas*, reduce inflammation, and promote overall health.

A traditional therapy involves soaking three untreated Pancha Mukhi beads overnight in a copper vessel and drinking the water, which is believed to help regulate blood pressure, diabetes, and kidney ailments.

Mantras for Pancha Mukhi Rudraksha:

Om Namah Shivaya

Om Hreem Namah

Om Hoom Namah

Om Hreem Hoom Namah

Mahamrityunjaya Mantra

6 Mukhi Rudraksha

The six-faced Rudraksha is one of the more common and affordable types of beads. The ones from Nepal are similar in size to the five-faced Rudraksha, while the Indonesian varieties tend to be smaller, usually between 8 mm and 10 mm in diameter.

The energy of the 6 Mukhi Rudraksha is connected to Lord Kartikeya, a form of Lord Shiva, symbolizing courage, confidence, and spiritual growth. This bead is easily available and is a budget-friendly choice.

Wearing the 6 Mukhi Rudraksha is believed to bring wealth, good health, and happiness. Medicinally, it is said to help with urinary problems, neck issues, eye disorders, and sexual health. Additionally, wearing it on the right wrist or arm may aid those who struggle with speech defects such as stammering.

This Rudraksha is especially recommended for students, teachers, artists, writers, scientists involved in mental work, as well as leaders and actors who frequently perform or speak publicly.

Mantras for 6 Mukhi Rudraksha:

Om Namah Shivaya

Om Hreem Hoom Namah

Om Hoom Namah

Om Hroom

Om Hreem Namah

Mahamrityunjaya Mantra

7 Mukhi Rudraksha

The seven-faced Rudraksha is almost perfectly round. The Indonesian version is smaller, generally around 8 mm to 10 mm across. Though less common than the six-faced variety, it is still fairly accessible.

This bead is linked to Ananta — the supreme Lord Brahma, who is limitless and infinite. The 7 Mukhi Rudraksha represents the Sapta

Rishis (seven sages) who bless the wearer with health, wealth, the removal of obstacles, and overall growth in life.

It is traditionally believed to help control arthritis, muscular pain, throat diseases, and even leukemia.

Mantras for 7 Mukhi Rudraksha:

Om Namah Shivaya

Om Hum Namah

Om Hrah

Om Hreem Namah

Om Hreem Shreem Kreem Soam

Mahamrityunjaya Mantra

8 Mukhi Rudraksha

The Nepalese version of this bead has a slightly oval shape, while the Indonesian type tends to be smaller, ranging from 9 mm to 15 mm in diameter. Compared to the 7 Mukhi Rudraksha, the 8 Mukhi is much rarer and significantly more expensive — costing about 10 to 20 times as much.

This Rudraksha is associated with Lord Ganesha, the remover of obstacles, who symbolizes wisdom, knowledge, and spiritual growth. Due to its rarity and powerful symbolism, the 8 Mukhi Rudraksha is highly valued.

It is believed to enhance intelligence, analytical thinking, understanding, and writing skills. Medically, it is thought to aid nervous system disorders, prostate issues, and gall bladder problems.

Mantras for 8 Mukhi Rudraksha:

Om Namah Shivaya

Om Hum Namah

Om Sah Hoom Namah

Om Kam Vam Namah

Mahamrityunjaya Mantra

Om Hreem Greem Hem

Aam Shreem

9 Mukhi Rudraksha

The nine-faced Rudraksha is relatively uncommon and can be found in Nepal and Indonesia. It is more oval and flatter than the 8 Mukhi Rudraksha, and it tends to be more expensive.

This bead is connected to several deities, including Lord Bhairava, Goddess Shakti (in her nine forms), and Yamraj, the god of death. Wearing it is said to help overcome fears, especially the fear of death, making the wearer more confident and fearless.

Mantras for 9 Mukhi Rudraksha:

Om Namah Shivaya

Om Hreem Namah

Om Hum Namah

Om Sum

Om Hreem Veing Yun

Raim Laim

Mahamrityunjaya Mantra

10 Mukhi Rudraksha

The ten-faced Rudraksha is linked to Lord Vishnu and the Dashdigpalas — guardians of the ten directions. Although rarer than the 9 Mukhi, it is relatively affordable.

This Rudraksha is recommended for business people, those involved in legal disputes, and anyone facing professional or career struggles. It is also said to help with insomnia and mental stress.

Mantras for 10 Mukhi Rudraksha:

Om Namah Shivaya

Om Hreem Namah Namah

Om Hreem Namah

Om Ksheem

Mahamrityunjaya Mantra

11 Mukhi Rudraksha

Also known as the Ekadasha Rudraksha, this bead is associated with Lord Hanuman, the symbol of courage and strength.

Wearing the 11 Mukhi Rudraksha is believed to increase self-confidence, physical strength, and oratory skills. It enhances leadership qualities and helps control the senses, making it popular for meditation and spiritual practices.

It is also said to help with stomach disorders, acidity, liver and breast diseases, heart ailments, diabetes, and blood pressure.

Mantras for 11 Mukhi Rudraksha:

Om Namah Shivaya

Om Hreem Hum Namah

Om Shreem Namah

Om Shreem

Om Room Moom Yoom Aum

Mahamrityunjaya Mantra

Through these descriptions, we see how each Rudraksha face, from the single Mukhi to the eleven Mukhi, is tied to a specific deity and carries unique energetic qualities. This ancient wisdom, backed by spiritual and scientific insights, continues to provide comfort and guidance to many across the world.

Chapter 5 – Choosing the Right Rudraksha

Now that you've learned how Rudraksha beads work and the energies they carry, you might be wondering: How do I know which Rudraksha is the perfect one for me? Choosing the right Rudraksha is incredibly important because the right bead can help you grow spiritually, emotionally, and in many other areas of your life.

Beware of Fake Rudrakshas

Unfortunately, the market today is flooded with fake and artificial Rudraksha beads. Many sellers focus only on profit, ignoring the sacred spiritual value these beads hold. Some dishonest people glue beads together, carve fake faces on ordinary seeds, or sell identical-looking fake beads. It's crucial to know how to check the authenticity of Rudrakshas before buying or wearing one.

Studies and expert reports suggest that for every genuine Rudraksha, there might be three or four fake ones circulating in the market. Some sources even estimate that up to 40% of Rudrakshas sold are entirely fake, and another 40% are artificially altered. This means only about 10-20% of what you find might be authentic! Sadly, many traditional sellers don't share clear ways to spot real Rudraksha beads, possibly because it could affect their business.

Surprisingly, while there are plenty of books full of mantras, prayers, and stories about Rudraksha, there isn't a widely known guide specifically designed to help buyers distinguish real beads from fake ones. Plus, some special Rudrakshas, like the rare Trijuti or beads with 14 or more faces, are often counterfeited with skillful tricks —

including cleverly joining smaller pieces inside the bead to mimic the natural pattern.

Why Is It So Hard to Identify a Genuine Rudraksha?

Right now, there's no easy machine or device that anyone can use to check a Rudraksha's authenticity. Since these beads are natural seeds, their size, shape, and internal structure vary depending on where they come from. The subtle electromagnetic energy they supposedly carry is too faint and inconsistent for reliable scientific measurement. So, even if scientists tried to set standards, the results would likely be unclear or inaccurate.

People often use several traditional methods to test a Rudraksha, but most of these are not foolproof. Let's take a closer look at some popular tests and why they may not always work.

Common Tests & Why They May Not Always Work

Does it sink in water?
A ripe Rudraksha seed is usually denser than water, so it should sink — that sounds simple, right? But here's the catch: many fake beads also sink because scammers glue beads or add heavy materials like metal or glass inside lighter objects. Some clever fraudsters even use light seeds or wood stuffed with heavy stuff to trick this test.

So, while a genuine Rudraksha typically sinks, sinking alone doesn't guarantee it's real. Also, if your Rudraksha has a big hollow inside, it may trap air and float for a while before sinking. Sometimes, dry or unripe beads float too. When testing, it's best to remove beads from necklaces and test each separately.

Does it rotate between copper coins?
Some say holding a Rudraksha between two copper coins will make it rotate due to its electromagnetic energy. Actually, any small round object with bumps can spin when pressed between coins because of friction — even ordinary seeds. This has nothing to do with energy and can't reliably prove authenticity.

The pendulum or palm test
Energy healers sometimes use pendulums or their hands to sense vibrations or energy fields around Rudrakshas. While these skills can be fascinating, most scientific experts don't consider them reliable for testing Rudraksha genuineness.

Boiling in milk
Some say boiling a Rudraksha in milk preserves the milk longer or has healing effects. While the bead might alter the milk's electrical properties slightly, there's no scientific proof that this test works to verify a Rudraksha.

Other odd tests
You might hear strange tests, like placing a one-faced Rudraksha in rice or under leaves overnight, expecting it to rise magically. These are myths, and none have real scientific backing.

Common Tests & Why They May Not Always Work		
Test	**Description**	**Why It May Not Always Work**
Does it sink in water?	Genuine Rudraksha seeds are usually denser than water, so it should sink — that sounds simple, right?	Fake beads may also sink due to stuffing materials or heavy wool stuffing; rotation to energy and doesn't isn't proof
Does it rotate between copper coins?	Holding the bead between two copper coins to see if it rotates, supposedly due to electromagnetic energy	No scientific evidence supports this as a test for authenticity; any as ere minimal and not conducisie
The pendulum or palm test	Using a pendulum or palm to sense vibrations or energy fields aruund the bead	Myths without scientifically backing and do not verify authenticity
Boiling in milk	Boiling Rudraksha in milk is believed to preserve a	Myths without scientifically backing and do not verify authenticity
Other odd tests	You might hear strange tests, like placing a Rudraksha in rice	These are myths, and none have real scientific backing

What Really Matters When Choosing Your Rudraksha

The most important part is to pick a Rudraksha you feel **connected to**. It's your personal journey, and the bead that resonates with you will help you most.

Here are some key points to guide you:

- **Know your needs:** What do you want to improve in your life? Is it financial success, spiritual growth, peace of mind, or better health? Understanding your priorities will help you choose the right Rudraksha.
- **Consult an expert:** A knowledgeable guide can recommend the best Rudraksha for your personality, lifestyle, and goals. Remember, each Rudraksha has its unique qualities.
- **Check for quality:** Invest in a genuine, high-quality Rudraksha. It might cost more, but it lasts longer and offers more benefits.
- **Prepare your Rudraksha:** Before wearing your bead, cleanse it with pure water and energize it by placing it in sunlight or moonlight. This process activates the bead's energy and helps you bond with it.

Chapter 6 – Purification and Activation of the Rudraksha

Before you start wearing a Rudraksha mala or a collection of beads, there are some important steps to follow to ensure you receive their full spiritual and energetic benefits. These simple checks and preparations create a respectful connection between you and your Rudraksha.

- **Check the number and condition:** Make sure your mala has the correct number of beads. Also, the Rudraksha beads should be brand new — never worn or used by anyone else. They should be free from any cracks, holes, or damage to preserve their energy.
- **Proper stringing:** The beads in your mala should be strung carefully, with all the "faces" (the natural lines or mukhis on the beads) pointing in the same direction, and the "tails" opposite. This alignment is believed to help the energy flow uniformly through the beads.
- **Cleanse your body:** Before wearing the Rudraksha, it's best to cleanse yourself by taking a bath or shower. This physical purification is thought to prepare your mind and body to receive the spiritual energies of the beads more effectively.
- **Choose the right day:** Monday is considered the most auspicious day to begin wearing your Rudraksha. Starting on this day is said to enhance the bead's spiritual power throughout your week.

Guidelines for Wearing Rudraksha

Check the number and condition
Ensure your Rudraksha mala has the correct number of new, undamaged beads. They should be unused to preserve their energy.

Proper stringing
Take a bath or shower before wearing the Rudraksha.

Cleanse your body
Cleanse yourself (bath/shower) before wearing Rudraksha to better receive its spiritual energy.

Choose the right day
Monday is the most auspicious day to start wearing your Rudraksha, believed to enhance its spiritual power for the week.

Wear an odd number of beads
For enhanced energy, wear an odd number (1, 3, 5, 7, or 9) of Rudraksha beads.

Remove the Rudraksha at certain times
Avoid wearing Rudraksha during impure activities or menstruation; purify with water and "Om Namah Shivaya" if accidentally worn.

Complete the payment
Always ensure your Rudraksha is fully paid for; unpaid or stolen beads are believed to weaken their energy and bring negativity.

Avoid others touching your beads
Never share or let others touch your Rudraksha beads, as they absorb energy that could interfere with their spiritual influence.

Open to all religion
Rudraksha is a spiritual topol accessible to everyone, regardless of religious background

No negative side effects
No harm comes from wearing Rudraksha; it's for lifelong spiritual growth, not instant miracles.

- **Wear an odd number of beads:** When wearing multiple Rudraksha beads, it is ideal to choose an odd number such as 1, 3, 5, 7, or 9. Odd numbers are traditionally considered more sacred and powerful, helping to amplify the positive vibrations of the Rudraksha.
- **Remove the Rudraksha at certain times:** Avoid wearing your Rudraksha when consuming alcohol, eating meat, during intimate moments, and at funerals. Additionally, women are advised to remove them during their menstrual cycle. If you forget and wear them during these times, don't worry — just purify your beads afterward by washing them with clean water and chanting "Om Namah Shivaya" five times.
- **Complete the payment:** Always ensure you have fully paid for your Rudraksha mala or beads. According to traditional belief, if the beads aren't fully purchased (except as a gift), their energy may weaken, and you might even experience negative feelings or doubts. Importantly, never use stolen Rudraksha beads.
- **Avoid others touching your beads:** Rudraksha beads absorb energy from anyone who handles them. This could interfere with their intended spiritual influence. For this reason, it's best not to share your beads or allow others to touch them.
- **Open to all religions:** Rudraksha is a spiritual tool accessible to everyone, regardless of religious background.

Rituals are optional and should always be done with respect and genuine intention.

- **No negative side effects:** Wearing Rudraksha beads doesn't cause harm. Don't worry about any harmful effects, and don't expect instant miracles. Wearing Rudraksha is meant to be a lifelong journey of spiritual growth and healing.
- **Use only new or purified beads:** Always use new Rudraksha beads that no one else has worn. If you inherit or receive beads from loved ones, cleanse them first using purification rituals like Abhishek. Check old beads carefully for damage — beads with cracks or holes should not be used.

Ancient scriptures emphasize the importance of worshipping your Rudraksha regularly, especially by chanting mantras. The *Shrimad Devibhagawat* advises wearing Rudraksha with devotion and happiness, without expecting specific outcomes, to gain the true knowledge of Lord Shiva. Even wearing Rudraksha without chanting is beneficial, but for Brahmins or those following Brahmin traditions, mantra chanting is essential. The *Shiva Puran* praises those who chant special "beej" mantras while wearing Rudraksha, saying even hearing these mantras brings blessings.

Preparing for Activation

Before you activate your Rudraksha beads—unlocking their full spiritual energy—it's important to prepare both your surroundings and yourself.

- **Conditioning the beads:** New Rudraksha beads should be soaked first in pure ghee for 24 hours, then in full-fat milk for another 24 hours. After soaking, rinse them with clean water. This process softens the beads and prepares them for activation.
- **Stringing method:** Traditional texts suggest stringing Rudraksha beads so that the opening (face) of one bead faces the opening of the next, and the tails align similarly. This arrangement keeps beads evenly spaced and creates a visually and energetically balanced mala.
- **Purifying the beads:** Begin the activation by washing the beads with *Gangajal* (holy Ganges water), which purifies the beads spiritually. Then soak them in a mixture of ghee and milk, further increasing their divine energy.

After this careful preparation, your Rudraksha beads will be ready to wear and connect with your personal energy.

Blessing Your Rudraksha (Simple Method)

If you want to bless your Rudraksha before wearing it, follow this straightforward ritual, best done on an auspicious day like Monday or any day you feel drawn to:

1. Wash the Rudraksha bead or mala with Ganges water or clean water.
2. Apply a small amount of sandalwood paste to the bead(s).
3. Light incense or dhoop (fragrant smoke) and offer it to the Rudraksha.
4. Offer a white flower to the beads.
5. Touch the Rudraksha to a *Shivalingam* (symbolic representation of Lord Shiva) or an image of Lord Shiva while chanting "Om Namah Shivaya" at least 11 times.
6. After this ritual, you can wear the Rudraksha or place it in your worship area.

The knots between each bead symbolize the union of two energies. To honor this, each knot should be made sacred during stringing by chanting "Om" slowly and with intention. Traditionally, the person stringing the mala is knowledgeable and devout, reciting "Om" for each of the 108 knots. This makes the mala truly blessed.

Rudraksha Abhishek (Elaborate Blessing Ritual)

For a deeper, more formal blessing, the *Abhishek* ritual can be performed by you, your guru, or a priest. It requires some special items:

- **Washing materials:** Either *Panchgavya* (a mixture of cow dung, urine, milk, ghee, and curd) or *Panchamrit* (milk, honey, sugar, ghee, and curd).

- **Ganges water and kusha grass** for sprinkling.
- **Nine Peepal tree leaves** arranged on a plate (optional).
- **Offerings:** Incense, camphor, sandalwood paste, aromatic oils, rice grains mixed with fragrant powder (*ashtagandha* if available), a ghee lamp, cloth, flowers, fruit, betel nut, betel leaves, and coconut.

How to Perform Rudraksha Worship (Puja) Step-by-Step

Once you have everything ready for the Rudraksha puja:

1. Take a bath, clear your mind, and sit facing east on a mat or a clean carpet.
2. Wash the Rudraksha bead with Panchgavya or Panchamrit (a sacred mixture of five products from the cow).
3. Then wash it again with clean water, preferably from the Ganges.
4. Place the Rudraksha on a plate, optionally with Peepal leaves.
5. Put an empty plate in front of you for offerings.
6. Chant "Om Namah Shivaya" three times to invoke Lord Shiva's blessings.
7. Sprinkle water on yourself and all ritual items while chanting this cleansing mantra:

"Om Apavitrah Pavitro va sarva Vastan Gatopi Va Yah smaret Pundari Kaksham Sa Bahya Bhyantarah Shuchih."

8. Chant the following names three times to honor your spiritual guides and deities:

   "Om gurubhyo namaha, Om Ganeshaya namaha, Om kula devatabhya namaha, Om ishta devatabhya namaha, Om mata pitribhyam namaha."

9. After chanting each of these three names, take a sip of water from your right hand (using a spoon or a small pot):

   "Om Keshavaya namaha, Om Narayana namaha, Om Madhavaya namaha."

10. Pour a little water from your right hand onto the ground while chanting:

    "Om Govindaya namaha."

11. Perform three short breathing exercises (pranayama) to calm the mind and body.

12. Chant the mantra:

    "Om pranavasya parabrahma rishihi paramatma devata daivi Gayatri chandaha pranayamae viniyogaga."

13. Sprinkle water on the Rudraksha with kusa grass or a spoon while chanting:

"Om Sadyojatam prapadyaami sadyajataajava namo namaha Bhave bhavenaati bhave bhaavasvamaan bhavodbhavay namaha."

14. Take a flower dipped in sandalwood paste and aromatic oils, and touch it to the Rudraksha while chanting:

    "Om Vamdevaya namaha, jyeshthaay namaha shreshthay namaha, Rudraay namah, kaalay namah, Kala vikarannaay namah, Bal vikaranaay namah, Balaay namah, Bala pramathanaay namah, Sarva bhoot damanaay namah, Manomanaay namah."

15. Offer incense smoke (dhup) to the Rudraksha while chanting:

    "Om Aghorebhyo ghorebhyo ghor ghor tarebhayaha Sarvebhya sarva sharvvebhyo namaste astu Rudra roopebhyaha."

16. Again, take a flower dipped in sandalwood paste and touch it to the beads while chanting:

    "Om Tatpurushaaya vidmahe Mahadevaay dheemahi tanno Rudraha prachodayaat."

17. Chant the Eeeshan mantra:

    "Om Eeeshan sarvavidyaanam eeshwar sarvabhootaanaam Brahnaadipati brahmanaadhipati Brahma Shivome astu sadaa Shivom."

18. Chant the Pranpratishtha mantra to give life to the bead. While chanting, offer rice grains into the empty plate:

    "Om aam hreem krom yum rum lum vum shum shum sum haum hum sah asya malaya prana eha prana. Om aam hreem krom yum

rum lum vum shum shum sum haum hum sah asya malaya jeeva eha sthitha Om aam hreem krom yum rum lum vum shum shum sum haum hum sah asya malaya sarveindrayani vagmansyachakshu shodragranapadani ihevagatya sukham chiram thithantu swaha."

Specific Offerings to Lord Shiva

Next, chant these mantras while offering corresponding items (or rice if the item is unavailable) onto the plate:

- **Invocation:**

  "Avahanam samarpayami Shri Shiva Maha Devaya charana kamalebhyo namaha" (I offer this invocation to the lotus feet of Lord Shiva.)

- **Seat:**

  "Asanam samarpayami Shri Shiva Maha Devaya charana kamalebhyo namaha" (I offer this seat to the lotus feet of Lord Shiva.)

- **Cloth:**

  "Vastram samarpayami Shri Shiva Maha Devaya charana kamalebhyo namaha" (I offer this cloth to the lotus feet of Lord Shiva.)

- **Sandalwood/Scent:**

"Chandanam samarpayami Shri Shiva Maha Devaya charana kamalebhyo namaha" (I offer sandalwood paste or scent to the lotus feet of Lord Shiva.)

- **Rice:**

  "Akshatan samarpayami Shri Shiva Maha Devaya charana kamalebhyo namaha" (I offer unbroken rice grains.)

- **Flower:**

  "Pushpam samarpayami Shri Shiva Maha Devaya charana kamalebhyo namaha" (I offer a flower.)

- **Ghee Lamp:**

  "Deepam samarpayami Shri Shiva Maha Devaya charana kamalebhyo namaha" (I offer the ghee lamp.)

- **Water for Washing Hands:**

  "Achamaniyam samarpayami Shri Shiva Maha Devaya charana kamalebhyo namaha" (I offer water for washing hands.)

- **Fruit:**

  "Naivedyam samarpayami Shri Shiva Maha Devaya charana kamalebhyo namaha" (I offer fruit.)

- **Water for Drinking:**

  "Achamaniyam samarpayami Shri Shiva Maha Devaya charana kamalebhyo namaha" (I offer water for drinking.)

- **Betel Nut (Paan):**

"Tambulam samarpayami Shri Shiva Maha Devaya charana kamalebhyo namaha" (I offer betel nut.)

- **Coconut:**

"Shriphalam samarpayami Shri Shiva Maha Devaya charana kamalebhyo namaha" (I offer coconut.)

Final Steps

1. Burn camphor and circle it clockwise three times in front of the plate while chanting:

   "Karpura Shivam karuna vataram samsara saram bhujagendra haram Sada vasantam hridaya ravinde bhavam bhavani sahitam namami" (I bow to Shiva, pure as camphor, embodiment of compassion, essence of the world, wearing the king of snakes as garland, always residing in the heart with Bhavani.)

2. Chant the Gayatri mantra three times:

   "Om bhur bhuvesh swaha Om tat saviturvarenyum bhargo devasya dheemahi dhiya yonaha prachodayat."

3. Chant the Surya (Sun) mantra three times, touching your right eye, left eye, and forehead after each part:

   "Om bhu bhuwaha, om swaha, om maha, om janaha, om tapaha, om satyam Om apo jyothi Raso amtritam Brahma bhu bhuwaha swarom."

4. Chant the Mahamrityunjaya mantra five times, offering rice to the plate after each round:

   "Om Haum Joom Sah, Om Bhur Bhuvaha Swaha, Om Tryambakam Yajamahey Sungandhim Pushti Vardanam, Urvarukamiva Bandhanan, Mrityor Muksheeya Mamritat, Om Swaha Bhuvaha Bhu Om Sah Joom Haum Om."

5. Chant the Beeja (seed) mantras nine times each:

   "Om Namah Shivaya, Om Hreem Namah, Om Namah, Om Kleem Kleem Namah, Om Hreem Namah, Om Hreem Hum namah, Om Hum Namah, Om Kraum Kshom Rom Namah."

6. Bow down or offer your prayers, then chant this final peace prayer:

   "Om Purnamadah Purnamidam Purnat Purnamudachyate, Purnasya Purnamadaya Purna Mevavya Shishyate Om Shantih Shantih Shantih!"

While different texts may vary slightly, this ritual is considered a comprehensive way to fully energize and sanctify your Rudraksha beads, connecting you deeply to their spiritual essence.

Chanting Mantras for Activation

Mantra chanting is vital in awakening the Rudraksha's powers. Here's a list of recommended mantras for each type of Rudraksha bead based on the number of *mukhis* (faces):

Mukhi Number Mantra

Mukhi Number	Mantra
One	Om Hreem Namah
Two	Om Namah
Three	Om Kleem Namah
Four	Om Hreem Namah
Five	Om Hreem Namah
Six	Om Hreem Hoom Namah
Seven	Om Hoom Namah
Eight	Om Hoom Namah
Nine	Om Hreem Hoom Namah
Ten	Om Hreem Namah Namah
Eleven	Om Hreem Hoom Namah
Twelve	Om Krom Kshom Roam Namah
Thirteen	Om Hreem Namah
Fourteen	Om Namah

Maintenance and Care

To preserve the energy and physical condition of your Rudraksha beads, proper maintenance is essential:

- **Condition every six months:** Soak your beads again in ghee and milk to nourish and protect them. This conditioning helps keep the beads strong and spiritually potent.
- **Managing oiliness:** After conditioning, if the beads feel oily, gently dust them with *Vibhuti* (sacred ash) to remove excess oil.
- **Daily cleaning:** Avoid harsh chemical soaps or cleaners. Instead, soak your beads overnight in mild soap water and rinse them the next day with a clean, soft cloth.
- **Storage:** Store your Rudraksha beads in natural containers like wooden boxes, glass jars, or clay pots. Avoid plastic containers, which can affect the beads negatively. If you don't wear your beads for a long time, keep them wrapped in a soft silk cloth to maintain their purity and energy.

Wearing and caring for Rudraksha beads with devotion, respect, and patience connects you to ancient spiritual wisdom. Over time, this bond nurtures your mind, body, and soul, guiding you on your path toward balance, peace, and inner strength.

Chapter 7 – Rudraksha and Yoga

The connection between Rudraksha and yoga is a deeply rooted relationship centered on one vital concept: life force energy, also known in Sanskrit as prana. In the ancient Indian yogic tradition, Rudraksha is more than just a sacred seed—it is considered a spiritual conductor, channeling pranic energy to elevate both physical and mental well-being.

Rudraksha acts as a spiritual companion to the yogi. Whether you're a spiritual seeker, a student of yoga, or someone simply exploring mindfulness, Rudraksha is seen as a beacon of positive energy that can guide you inward, helping you tap into the true potential of your inner self.

How Rudraksha Complements Yogic Practice

Yoga is not just a series of physical postures; it is a holistic system that includes asana (posture), pranayama (breathwork), dhyana (meditation), and samadhi (deep absorption). When combined with Rudraksha, each of these stages becomes more aligned and energetically supported:

RUDRAKSHA AND YOGA

1. Rudraksha During Asanas (Postures)

While physical postures focus on flexibility, strength, and body alignment, wearing Rudraksha—especially around the neck or wrist—can help ground your energy, keeping your nervous system calm and your mind centered. Its bio-electric properties interact subtly with the body's magnetic field, promoting balance and endurance during yoga sessions.

2. Rudraksha During Pranayama (Breath Control)

Pranayama aims to regulate and expand life force through the breath. Rudraksha beads are believed to help stabilize the flow of prana by calming the breath and reducing distractions. Wearing them during breathwork is said to lower stress levels and deepen the practitioner's awareness of inner rhythms.

3. Rudraksha in Meditation and Dhyana

This is where the power of Rudraksha truly shines. The beads serve as tools for mantra chanting (japa) and help in counting breaths or repetitions without losing focus. Rudraksha encourages a state of stillness and detachment, helping the meditator transcend the noise of the mind and move into a space of inner silence and presence.

4. Rudraksha and Chakras

Yogic practices often involve the chakra system—the energy centers of the body. Different types of Rudraksha beads are associated with different chakras. For example:

- 1 Mukhi Rudraksha is linked with the Sahasrara (Crown) Chakra—ideal for deep meditation and enlightenment.

- 5 Mukhi Rudraksha balances the Vishuddha (Throat) Chakra—improving communication and inner truth.
- 6 and 7 Mukhi beads align with lower chakras, promoting emotional balance and grounding.

By choosing Rudraksha beads aligned with the chakras you want to work on, your yogic practice becomes more focused and energetically attuned.

Scientific Perspective in Yoga Practice

Modern science has shown that Rudraksha beads possess electromagnetic and inductive properties that can influence alpha brain waves, heart rate, and blood circulation. These physiological effects support the core goals of yoga—balance, relaxation, and heightened awareness.

Some studies suggest that Rudraksha helps regulate the heartbeat and blood pressure, especially during deep breathing and meditative practices—making it an ideal natural accessory for a yoga practitioner aiming to enhance both health and spiritual vitality.

Types of Rudraksha Suitable for Yogis

Certain types of Rudraksha are particularly recommended for yoga practitioners:

- **5 Mukhi (Five-faced)**: The most commonly used; represents Lord Shiva, brings peace and clarity—ideal for everyday yoga and meditation.
- **6 Mukhi**: Associated with Kartikeya; supports focus and discipline.
- **7 Mukhi**: Invokes Lakshmi and Shiva; helps in overcoming internal fears and emotional instability.
- **11 Mukhi**: Known to enhance meditative depth and protect energy during intense spiritual practices.

Wearing these Rudraksha beads during yoga can help enhance energy alignment, protect your aura, and strengthen spiritual focus.

Mindfulness, Energy, and the Present Moment

In the modern world, distractions are everywhere. Yoga and Rudraksha together offer a method to return to the now. The tactile feeling of moving Rudraksha beads between your fingers during meditation or while sitting in Sukhasana (easy pose) serves as a reminder to stay grounded, present, and aware.

Even teenagers who are new to yoga can benefit from Rudraksha. It helps bring calmness during exams, improve concentration during study time, and reduce anxiety through consistent use in breathing exercises or mindfulness sessions.

Using Rudraksha Mindfully in Yoga Practice

If you're incorporating Rudraksha into your yoga routine, consider the following tips:

- **Wear the mala or bracelet during your practice** (unless it restricts movement).
- **Use the Rudraksha mala to guide breath count or mantra chanting** during Pranayama and Dhyana.
- **Store your beads respectfully**—keep them clean, sacred, and away from negative environments.
- **Choose the Rudraksha that aligns with your personal goals**—peace, focus, energy, or inner strength.

Conclusion: A Powerful Union of Ancient Wisdom

Rudraksha and yoga are two timeless gifts from ancient Indian wisdom. When practiced together, they do more than improve your physical health—they help you discover a deeper meaning to life, a connection to the divine, and most importantly, a closer relationship with yourself.

So whether you are rolling out your mat for the first time or you're deep in your spiritual path, let Rudraksha be your silent supporter—anchoring your breath, lifting your spirit, and guiding your energy toward peace and transformation.

Chapter 8 – Meditation with Rudraksha

Rudraksha prayer beads, commonly known as *malas*, are traditionally used for spiritual practices like chanting and meditation. Among the different types, the five-faced Rudraksha (*Panchmukhi*) is most widely used for meditation, thanks to its accessibility and moderate energy levels suitable for general use. These beads come in a variety of sizes, but ones measuring about 7 to 10 millimetres are considered ideal. They're easy to hold and comfortable to count with your fingers during chanting.

Understanding the Jap Mala

A typical *Jap Mala*—used for chanting mantras—has 108 beads plus one extra, known as the Meru Mani or Meru bead. This additional bead marks the start and end of one full round of chanting. You never cross the Meru bead while counting; instead, you reverse direction and continue. The significance of 108 lies in its spiritual symbolism—it represents the universe, the wholeness of existence, and the connection between the seeker and the divine.

Some malas are available in smaller sizes too:

- 54 + 1 beads
- 27 + 1 beads

These are convenient for shorter meditation sessions or for beginners who may find a full round of 108 beads overwhelming at first.

Types of Special Rudraksha Malas

Special malas can also be created by combining Rudraksha with metals:

- **Gold + Rudraksha:** This *Hariharatmika Mala* symbolizes the union of Lord Shiva and Lord Vishnu.
- **Silver + Rudraksha:** Represents the energies of Lord Shiva and Lord Brahma.

Such combinations carry dual spiritual benefits and are often used in more specific or advanced spiritual practices.

The Practice of Jap Yog (Chanting with a Mala)

Chanting mantras while rotating the beads of a mala is called Jap Yog—a practice that connects your body, mind, and soul through sound vibration. According to Lord Krishna in the Bhagavad Gita, Jap is one of the highest and most effective forms of yoga.

How to use the Mala for chanting:

- Hold the mala in your right hand.
- Use your thumb and middle finger to rotate the beads gently, pulling each bead toward you.
- Avoid using your index finger—this finger represents ego and should not interfere with your spiritual practice.

- When you reach the Meru bead, stop. Do not cross over it. Instead, reverse the mala and continue your next round in the opposite direction.
- Some people keep count of rounds by making marks with a pen or by placing separate counting beads on the side.

Dedicated Malas for Deities

Traditionally, different malas are used depending on which deity you're invoking:

Deity	**Recommended Mala**
Vishnu	Shankhmala (Conch beads)
Shiva	Rudraksha Mala
Ganesh	Gajadant (Elephant tooth)
Sharabhshalav	Bhadraksha Mala
Surya (Sun)	Pravalmala (Coral beads)

Using the appropriate mala enhances the energetic connection with the deity you're worshipping.

Guidelines and Etiquette for Chanting with Rudraksha Mala

Practicing Jap with discipline and devotion is key to receiving the full benefits. Here are some important do's and don'ts:

- Do not touch the beads with your nails. Use only the soft part of your fingers.
- Only use your right hand to handle the mala during chanting.
- The beads should always move towards you, symbolizing divine energy flowing into your life.
- Keep your index finger extended and away from the mala.
- When not in use, store your mala in a special cloth bag called a Gomukhi (cow's mouth bag) to protect and respect its sanctity.
- The mala should hang at heart level while chanting.
- Always place the image or symbol of the deity above the level of your mala to maintain respect.
- Face east for general spiritual practice, and keep your spine erect. Sitting in *Sukhasan* or *Padmasan* helps maintain posture and focus.
- Perform your chanting in the same place and at the same time daily to build spiritual discipline.

- Always cover your head during Jap for energetic containment.
- Focus on your Ajna Chakra (the point between your eyebrows) to deepen your concentration.
- Chant in one of three ways:
    - Silent (Manasik Jap): Most powerful, but requires strong focus.
    - Whispered (Upanshu Jap): Audible only to you.
    - Aloud (Vaikhari Jap): Good for beginners or group chanting.
- You can use a guru-given mantra, a personal mantra, or simply chant "Om."
- Don't mix up your chanting and wearing malas. Use different malas for each purpose.
- For counting rounds, use materials like red sandalwood, sindoor, lac, or cow dung balls as markers.

Direction Matters

The direction you face during Jap affects the energy you attract:

- **East:** General spiritual growth, divine connection, and sadhana.
- **North:** Peace, protection, mental clarity, and wisdom.

- **West:** Attract wealth and abundance.
- **South:** Used in tantric or transformative practices.

Construction of a Rudraksha Mala

The spiritual energy of a mala doesn't only come from its use, but also from the **way it is made**.

- Malas can be strung with cotton, silk, silver, copper, or gold.
- Red or black threads are commonly used.
- Each bead should be strung so that the "face" (mukhi) of one aligns with the face of the next, and the "tails" align as well. This preserves symmetry and energy flow.
- While stringing, the person should chant "Om" for each bead to energize and sanctify the mala.
- To prevent beads from rubbing or rotating:
    - Use larger knots (twice the size of the bead hole) between each bead if using thread.
    - Alternatively, use small metal loops or caps to separate beads on a wire.
- If you are using metal wire (especially with higher mukhi Rudraksha), insert wool thread inside the bead's hole. This reduces friction and protects these precious beads from wear and tear over years of use.

In Summary:

Meditating with Rudraksha is not just a practice—it is a sacred discipline that blends devotion, awareness, and universal connection. Whether you're a teenager beginning your journey or an adult deepening your spiritual roots, let the mala be your silent companion. With each bead you touch, you're not only reciting a sound—you're stepping closer to peace, awareness, and the divine within.

Acknowledgement

I would like to express my heartfelt gratitude to everyone who supported me throughout the journey of writing this book, *Beyond the Divine Beads.*

First and foremost, I am deeply indebted to my family, my parents, Dr. Pratap Mukherjee and Mrs. Jhimli Mukherjee and my friends for their unwavering love and encouragement. Their belief in me has been a constant source of motivation.

I would also like to thank the entire team at RidhzWorld Publishing for guiding me on this positive and purposeful path. Your insights, support, and encouragement have been instrumental in shaping this book. A special note of thanks to Samruddhi Naik for her thoughtful and meticulous editing.

Lastly, I extend my deepest appreciation to the countless seekers of spiritual wisdom whose curiosity and quest for knowledge inspired this journey. It is for you that I have poured my heart and soul into these pages, with the hope of illuminating your spiritual path through the sacred power of the Beyond The Divine Beads.

With deepest gratitude
Pragati Mukherjee